A Rainy Afternoon with God

Catherine B. Cawley

Paulist Press
New York/Mahwah, New Jersey

Cover/book design and interior illustrations by Nicholas T. Markell.

Copyright © 1998 by Catherine B. Cawley

Library of Congress Cataloging-in-Publication Data

Cawley, Catherine B.
   A rainy afternoon with God / by Catherine B. Cawley.
     p.   cm. — (IlluminationBooks)
   Includes bibliographical references.
   ISBN 0-8091-3779-8 (alk. paper)
   1. Retreats. 2. Cawley, Catherine B. I. Title. II. Series
BV5068.R4C35 1998
269′.6—dc21
                                        97-50235
                                          CIP

Published by Paulist Press
997 Macarthur Boulevard
Mahwah, New Jersey 07430

Printed and bound in the
United States of America

Contents

Acknowledgments

Writing this book would not have been possible without all those who support my work at Shalom House Retreat Center: the Catholic Diocese of Richmond's Bishop Walter F. Sullivan and countless individuals who generously volunteer their time to help Shalom House. Particular people took time to review my manuscript and make valuable suggestions: Pauline Flynn, Father Chester Michael, Peter and Judie Pudner, Carol Heiss, Sister Marie Kerns, Mae McKeon, Father Louis Benoit, Anne Hendrick, Audrey Stech, Pat Carreras, Helen Brolly, Florence Hartrim, Beth Ebner and Father Dennis Murphy. Thanks go especially to Bob Wicks for inviting me to write this book and encouraging me along the way.

–*Catherine B. Cawley*
Montpelier, Virginia

IlluminationBooks
A Foreword

When this series was launched in 1994, I wrote that Illumination-Books were conceived to "bring to light wonderful ideas, helpful information, and sound spirituality in concise, illustrative, readable, and eminently practical works on topics of current concern."

In keeping with this premise, among the first books were offerings by well-known authors Joyce Rupp *(Little Pieces of Light...Darkness and Personal Growth)* and Basil Pennington *(Lessons from the Monastery That Touch Your Life)*. In addition, there were titles by up-and-coming authors and experts in the fields of spirituality and psychology. These books covered a wide array of topics: joy, controlling stress and anxiety, personal growth, discernment, caring for others, the mystery of the Trinity, celebrating the woman you are, and facing your own desert experiences.

The continued goal of the series is to provide great ideas, helpful steps, and needed inspiration in small volumes. Each of the books offers a new opportunity for the reader to explore possibilities and embrace practicalities that can be employed in everyday life. Thus, among the new and noteworthy themes for readers to discover are these: how to be more receptive to the love in our lives, simple ways to structure a personal day of recollection, a creative approach to enjoy reading sacred scriptures, and spiritual and psychological methods of facing discouragement.

Like the IlluminationBooks before them, forthcoming volumes are meant to be a source of support—without requiring an inordinate amount of time or prior preparation. To this end, each small work stands on its own. The hope is that the information provided not only will be nourishing in itself but also will encourage further exploration in the area.

When we view the world through spiritual eyes, we appreciate that sound knowledge is really useful only when it can set the stage for *metanoia,* the conversion of our hearts. Each of the IlluminationBooks is designed to contribute in some small but significant way to this process. So, it is with a sense of hope and warm wishes that I offer this particular title and the rest of the series to you.

–*Robert J. Wicks*
General Editor, IlluminationBooks

Introduction

So strongly have I believed in the absolute need to take time out of our busy lives for rest and reflection, that four years ago I deliberately determined to leave the fast-paced living and working conditions of Washington, D.C. in order to put my life to use creating space and opportunity for retreats and retreatants. My quest for a place where I could do just this led me to a retreat house in rural central Virginia, Shalom House Retreat Center, sponsored by the Catholic Diocese of Richmond.

Over time, members of the Center's Programming Committee and I have developed and held dozens of workshops and retreats. The very first of these was our 1993 Fall Day of Reflection, planned and presented by a pastoral counseling colleague, Pauline Flynn, and me. Since that October, we have held daylong Days of Reflection during each change of the earth's seasons. These quarterly pauses encourage us and our participants to mark changes and renewals in ourselves at the same time that we observe nature's changing renewal process around us.

This little book is about creating your own special Day of Reflection—a day (or days) that I hope you will make happen over and over again in your life. *The suggestions herein are quite specific and meant only as starting points for you. Please tailor them to your own particular needs.* I would be happy to hear about different ways that you have structured a Day of Reflection and would be interested in incorporating your ideas in a future edition of this book.

Chapter One

Planning a Day of Reflection

What is a Day of Reflection?

For me, a Day of Reflection is an opportunity that I give myself to take time off from my usual schedule to consider ultimate questions relating to my life on earth as part of God's creation. I use these occasions to ask myself, "What is the purpose of my life? What is God's will for me? How am I carrying out God's will as I perceive it?" A Day of Reflection is a time when I seek balance by becoming more harmonized with myself spiritually, emotionally and even physically. It is a day of rest and renewal.

Others will define a Day of Reflection according to their own particular needs and desires. Since, to my knowledge, there is no commonly recognized definition for a Day of Reflection, such a day can therefore be individually tailored according to your specific needs. Keep in mind that you can also decide to experience either shorter or longer periods of time than a day, for example, *Hours* or *Days* of Reflection. Regardless of its length, however, the vital aspect of this occasion is that *it is time you've set aside from the regular hustle and bustle of your everyday, probably overscheduled, life.*

The prime purpose of a Day of Reflection is to *listen*. There are many things to listen *for* (e.g., God's voice or the wisdom of our own souls) and many things to listen "from" (e.g., Scripture or nature). Several activities and circumstances on a Day of Reflection facilitate listening. A description of these appears in chapter 2.

I think a big reason that relatively few people set aside time for a Day of Reflection is that the thought of doing so can be a little scary. They say to themselves, "Who am I to think I can structure a Day of Reflection? I have a hard enough time just dealing with day-to-day minor events. However could I devise a plan to fill a whole day?" If you find yourself saying similar things to yourself, I encourage you to read on.

Why should one even consider making a Day of Reflection?

The fact that you've been curious enough to pick up this book indicates some sort of inclination toward making a Day of Reflection. Perhaps there is some inner voice calling you to contemplation. Maybe it is something more simple, like your body sending you messages to slow down and take time to assess your life and where it's going. It may even be a realization that it is time to get perspective on a tough situation you're encountering or a recent crisis you've been through.

Unfortunately, societal forces lobby zealously against contemplation and inner reflection. This is because in the West, our culture strongly affirms "doing" and "action." We tend to feel less than "whole" if we're not busy every waking moment. How many "retired" people do you know who are busier than ever? For those of us who still work at full-time, paid jobs, any opportunity we once had to "get away from it all" has now been made nonexistent with the advent of cellular phones, modems, pagers, fax machines and laptop computers.

Indeed, the pace of life picks up without our even noticing it. Workers labor far more than forty hours a week as companies downsize, lay off some employees to cut costs and expect the remaining ones to assume more work and greater responsibilities. The sizes of cities and their outlying suburbs constantly increase, adding to our commuting time. For a long time, "labor-saving" devices have freed us from many chores, but now the use of appliances such as microwave ovens and automatic dishwashers provides a legitimate excuse for working overtime hours. Business travelers were once able to depend on travel time to get caught up on paperwork or even to enjoy some light reading. Now, however, trains, airplanes and rental cars are equipped with phones so that no one has an excuse for not checking in with the office during the course of the business day. All of these factors contribute to the sense that time is rushing by and that every minute must be filled with productive labor, for aren't most of us subscribers to the adage, "Time is money"?

The fact is that despite the tenets of our consumption-driven culture, the concept of time does not immediately translate into an element of monetary worth. Time is nothing more than a human device for ordering our days. Much too frequently, we spend so much time regretting the past and fearing the future that we completely lose sight of present time, the present moment, the time in which we truly live.

Present time is truly God's gift to us, and the best part is this: God doesn't place any expectation on us to accomplish anything of a particularly lofty nature with it. All God asks is that we live in accordance with those principles given to people long ago: love of God and neighbor. Thus, it is in the present moment that we meet God and that God is revealed to us, often through others.

In our lives today, it takes quite an effort of will to remove ourselves from life's so-apparently-important, tangible details in order to retreat to a place and time specially reserved for contemplation of those deeper, spiritual parts of ourselves. The value of doing so, however, can hardly be overstated.

A retreatant recently told me how she just about talked herself out of coming for her own special Weekend of Reflection. She felt that there were just too many more "important" and "timely" tasks at home. She wisely listened to her husband's insistence that she take this time for herself.

Aside from probably really needing it, another reason for deciding to undertake and carry out a Day of Reflection is that doing so is a wonderfully intimate and creative act. Designing a Day of Reflection is a way, a process to make one's faith and beliefs personal, not just a passive acceptance of "what others think." In addition, how often do we gift ourselves with a period of time that has no other demands upon it than that with which we want to fill it?

Who's involved in a Day of Reflection?

Who actually is involved in a Day of Reflection? Well, you, of course, are the necessary and prime participant. Be warned, however, that it may be a side of you with which you're a little unfamiliar that plays a leading part in your Day of Reflection. You will find that it is the more quiet, serious and thoughtful parts of your personality on which you will rely in planning and carrying out a worthwhile Day of Reflection. Nonetheless, your whole self will benefit from the experience.

The next chief player in this exercise is God. (Some people may find it more helpful to substitute a name such as Higher Power or Great Spirit.) God is the entity with whom we enter into relationship during a Day of Reflection.

Where and how individuals approach the wondrous Spirit of God through their Days of Reflection depend in part on what they seek. The following are some examples.

If it is the purpose of individuals on a Day of Reflection to praise and thank God for the beauties of creation, they should probably spend their time outdoors—in the mountains, at the beach, or even in their own backyards. Birdwatchers come to mind as some of the most grateful praisegivers on earth!

If the purpose is for individuals to discern direction at a particular time in their lives, they should seek a quiet, nondistracting place in which to encounter God.

Others may be seeking to know God, either initially or in a deeper way. At a certain point in most people's lives, they desire to set aside old and outgrown notions of God learned as children, and to seek a more mature image of their God. Perhaps they desire to develop their concept of God from one who punishes and abandons to one of a gentle, loving presence. These individuals may be drawn toward making a Day of Reflection at a retreat house where they would have access to religious and spiritual literature, as well as opportunity for discussion with a spiritual director.

While a group of people can certainly benefit from a Day of Reflection, greater growth in self-knowledge or knowledge of God is more apt to occur to individuals on a solitary Day of Reflection. Occasionally, it is appropriate to have another along, for example, a spouse or trusted friend—or even a child, whose vision and perspective would be quite refreshing. Nonetheless, the overall reason to set aside a Day of Reflection is to withdraw from the normal accompaniments of our day-to-day lives, including people!

Where should one make a Day of Reflection?

Once you've begun the planning process for a Day of Reflection, an important consideration that will arise is deciding the best location in which the day can take place.

At home. Since there is no need to make your Day of Reflection any more complicated than necessary, you might consider engaging in it at home. Perhaps there is a place in your house that you're particularly fond of: a bright sunroom, a darkened library or the alcove of a large room. The presence of candles or incense, as well as access to music on tape or CD, is certainly conducive to a Day of Reflection. If you decide to engage in your Day of Reflection at home, the kind of room and its furnishings are not nearly so important as the "feel" you have about a special place, which includes the extent to which the place contributes to quiet and peaceful relaxation.

Outside your home is another possibility. Perhaps you have the good fortune to live in a rural area surrounded by many acres of God's creation. A wooded setting or a spot alongside a pond or creek would make a good place for several hours of reflection. If the area around your home is small, even a garden setting would be a nice place to relax and enter into communion with God.

Away. While a Day of Reflection at home is good for some, many people find that *distance* from home is the main element that makes for a good Day of Reflection. Too often, the common surroundings of our lives provide exactly the distractions we don't need as we try to shed our normal routine so as to enter into the adventure of encountering God. The distance one goes from home does not have to be far, maybe just a few miles' drive to a state or city park. On the other hand, it appeals to some people to go much greater distances from home for their Days of Reflection. They feel that the drive itself of an hour or

more to and from a special location is a way of easing them into a new environment in which they will be truly open and receptive to hearing and responding to God's message.

Special places and circumstances. Someone I know engages in Days of Reflection at her summer home on the Chesapeake Bay. To meet her special purposes, she does not tightly structure her time there: she takes along some readings, including scriptures; she watches the water; and she works in her garden.

In thinking about *your* special place, it may help to spend some time in remembering a place or places in which, even as a child, you felt secure, cozy and whole. Such a place for me was curled up on the front porch glider of the home in which I grew up. I would go out there on a rainy afternoon, wrapped in a sweater, arms full of "light" reading—my comic books—and end up not reading but just sitting there, listening to the sound of rain on the porch roof, feeling the cool damp air. I loved those times, and while I then never came close to engaging in any form of prayer as I have come to know it, still I believe that during those quiet moments by myself, comfy in my physical experience of God's gifts of soft rain and cool air, my soul truly communed with our Creator and gave silent thanks for a chance to take time off from outdoor play activities and simply "be" in God's watchful presence.

In recent years, I have recaptured that intensely close-to-God feeling in other soft rain-drenched settings at unexpected times. A few years ago I returned to the retreat center after attending Sunday morning mass at my local parish. Our summer series of retreats had just ended that week. It was late August, the end of a fairly hot and dry summer; that particular day was cloudy, a little cooler, and before long, a soft rain began falling. Without even changing my Sunday clothes, I went and sat in the screened-in gazebo by the pond. My senses were alert and receptive: I heard the soft rain on the roof; I felt a gentle coolness in the slight breeze; I watched the rain, beginning to fall with some intensity, make a myriad of soft splashes on the pond's surface; and I smelled the freshness of the damp air. I sat there for hours, from time to time filling my coffee cup, but with no need for food, reading material or companionship. I thought of little. Instead, I just enjoyed *being* there, thanking God for the long-awaited weather shift, and luxuriating in that wondrous period of time.

While nearing the completion of this book, a friend and I took a day trip to a nearby monastery, Our Lady of the Angels, in Crozet, Virginia. We arrived in time for *sext* (one of the daily prayer times of the Church's liturgy of the hours). We asked if between the end of *sext* and the start of *none* we could take the lunch we had brought and eat it down at the base of the small mountain, where there was a little meditation garden, a pond and two cabins for retreatants. We learned that the cabins were closed for the winter and the gate to them was locked. We were told, however, that we could drive to see them anyway and were given the key to unlock the gate. The only problem was that when we arrived at the gate, we realized we'd mistakenly been given the wrong key. We knew we couldn't then return to the monastery, because the sisters were busy in the time immediately after *sext*.

We considered our options and decided to leave the car, climb the fence and walk in to where the cabins were. My friend took an umbrella from her car, since the day threatened rain. We walked along the gravel drive, noting little patches of unmelted snow, and passed two grazing cows. By the time we arrived in the vicinity of the cabins, the rain began and within minutes it was raining quite hard. We sought shelter, sitting on a stoop beneath the roof of the closest cabin. Sitting there, hearing the splash of rain on the boxwood leaves, listening to it tinkle on the cabin's tin roof and seeing the rain make rippling rings on the pond's surface, I relaxed and thoroughly enjoyed this little unplanned break. I shared with my friend previous times of feeling close to God in the experience of rain—sheltered from its wetness, yet still being outside, able to enjoy all aspects of its nature (except getting soaked!). She remarked that it was no accident Sister had mistakenly given us the wrong key. Had we driven in, we surely would have jumped back into the car when the rain came hard, thus altogether missing this wondrous encounter with God in the rain.

At a retreat house. An excellent location for a Day of Reflection is a retreat house, a place specifically designed for times to withdraw from the normal course of life. While some retreat houses engage in a specific urban ministry to the city in which they are located, most retreat houses are located in country settings, "far from the madding crowd," surrounded by acres of God's beautiful creation. Aside from their bounteous expanse of natural splendor, retreat houses also come well-equipped with different sorts of aids for reflective experience. Even small retreat houses are apt to contain books on a number of topics, musical or spoken tapes, prayer leaflets, meditation booklets, candles, a reading room and a chapel or prayer room. In addition, retreat houses are generally staffed by individuals with backgrounds in theology, prayer, spiritual direction or pastoral counseling.

Since, these days, many retreat houses derive most of their income from large weekend retreats that include overnight stays and meals, the best time to plan a quiet Day of Reflection there would probably be midweek.

Most retreat houses are affiliated with a particular religious denomination but rarely restrict their hospitality to people of their own faith tradition. The directors of most retreat houses happily welcome those who are seeking a deepening of their faith, as well as those who may be looking for a new perspective from which to encounter their God. (To learn the locations of retreat centers near you, contact your church, or one nearby; the pastor will gladly tell you the names and locations of nearby retreat centers with which he or she is familiar.)

How often does one need to take a Day of Reflection?

A simple answer to this question is: *as often as needed;* but, one asks, how often is that? Perhaps it's when the humdrum of life becomes so unchanging that you begin to lose sight of the wonder of your spouse and children or of the special joy of seeing a rainbow. When we find ourselves feeling unappreciative of God's abundant gifts, that is a good sign of our need to take time out to get in touch with our God.

Another clear sign of needing to slow down is the physical and emotional feelings of stress, an all-too-common sensation in our fast-paced, overcommitted lives. When one reaches the point where the treadmill of daily life is simply too fast and too steep, the most healthy approach is just to step off and take stock of what there is both too much of and too little of in one's life.

The anticipation of a major life change signals the need to take time out to reflect on God's will for you in the next stage of your earthly life. For example, it is not uncommon for pregnant women nearing the birth of their children to visit Shalom House for a period of time to reflect on their new (or enhanced) role as mother.

Working mothers, teachers, caregivers, and ministers of all types especially need regular opportunities to set aside time for refreshing themselves so that they may more fully reenter their lives of service to others. Recall how the gospels tell us that Jesus frequently needed to go away to a deserted place for prayer and rejuvenation.

Still another sign of needing to take a day to reflect is to feel almost the opposite of stressed, that is feeling bored—bored perhaps with the apparent meaninglessness of life's tasks or bored with shallow, sometimes insincere relationships.

It is even possible to be bored with an outgrown sense of God. In this regard, it may be necessary to replace an immature concept of God with a truer, more mature one. Oftentimes a sense of God was conveyed to one as a child, but this knowing of God has not been probed enough amidst the trials, cares and inconsistencies of adult

life, allowing it to grow into a relevant presence in our lives. We need to make opportunities to meet God with all our brokenness and cynicism and ask for God's healing balm.

Whether the motivation for a Day of Reflection be life's stress or boredom, at such times it is important to know that it is possible—even vital—to step out of everyday routines and begin to sow the seeds of our own re-creation, knowledgeable that with God we are indeed co-creators of both our destiny and the earthly path we take to achieve it. Want to reinvent your life? It's never too late! "With God, all things are possible" (Mt 19:26).

In reflecting on this particular urgency for a time of reflection, I am especially reminded of Isaiah's words, "All you who are thirsty, come to the water!...Why spend your money for what is not bread; your wages for what fails to satisfy?" (Is 55: 1–2). Yes, you can make a difference in the quality of your life!

Seasonal Days of Reflection. So convinced am I of the restorative effect of Days of Reflection, I strongly urge that they be taken regularly, for example, at least one day every three or four months. Those who live in climates in which seasonal changes are readily apparent have an excellent opportunity to pause at the beginning—or midpoint—of each season with a day off to "take stock" of themselves and to measure progress on their spiritual journey.

At Shalom House, we began marking the change of the earth's seasons every winter, spring, summer and fall as a way of observing growth and development in ourselves as we also note natural changes in the outdoor world around us.

When I first told the Catholic Diocese of Richmond's Bishop Walter Sullivan about our plans to initiate the program series of Shalom House with seasonal Days of Reflection, he responded by saying that these reminded him of the Church's once previously celebrated ember days. Ember days—three occurred each quarter—were days of prayer, fasting and reflection keyed to cycles of planting and harvesting. Like the ember days of an earlier time, we planned our seasonal Days of Reflection to be times to ponder our relationship to the universe and to hear God's voice speaking to us.

Should you decide to replicate our seasonal observations, the following are some themes and questions you might consider as you plan quarterly seasonal Days of Reflection:

• in winter, the season of dormancy, you might ask yourself, "For what am I preparing myself?";

• in spring, one comes alive and wonders, "Where does my energy need to be directed? In which productive—not random—channels?";

• in the lushness of summer, one asks, "Where and what are my growth areas? Which need pruning? Which need more tending?";

• in fall, the season of letting go, one asks, "What is it time to harvest? What habits do I need to let go of?"

Celebration of seasonal passages not only makes us accustomed to the necessity for frequent reflection, but also demonstrates to us, through nature's normal growth and dying cycles, ultimate life truths.

One of these truths is that change is a constant, regular part of life—nothing stays the same. The sight of the early spring flowers—crocuses, daffodils, forsythia—has caused someone I know to remark, "God is at work again."

Another ultimate life truth is that death is an inevitable, normal part of life. Everything in nature, ourselves included, comes from the earth and returns to the earth. People with close ties to the earth, for example, Native Americans or those from farming communities, know this intuitively.

The sad sight of bare tree limbs is but a temporary sight, for the advent of spring always brings budding blossoms. What a hopeful reminder this is for us in the cycle of our own temporary stay in this life and God's promise of our souls' resurrection.

Yearly Days of Reflection. Another way to schedule Days of Reflection is the marking of anniversaries. Anniversaries of deaths, in particular, call for a time of memory—a memorial—to the loved one no longer physically present in our earthly existence. In doing so, one might want to have at hand on the Day of Reflection the loved one's picture as a reminder of his or her life's contributions.

It is also important to recall the anniversary of lives never born: women need to mark the anniversary of miscarriages, stillbirths and abortions.

The observance of other anniversaries signaling marked changes in our relationships is likewise important: weddings, the births of our children, divorces and retirements.

Finally, anniversaries of special significance to

ourselves are not to be forgotten: our birthdays, leaving the home of our youth, the beginning of a chosen vocation, the initiation into our faith and so on.

In fact, to bestow a proper sense of dignity on these special days upon which one chooses to reflect, one might even look upon these (and others) as one's own set of sacred days. Both our traditional religions and our national governments so designate "holydays" and "holidays." We, too, have a right to our own special recognition of days that celebrate us and what is sacred to us in our lives as part of God's creation.

Preparation

At last you have realized the need for a Day of Reflection, chosen the time and selected the place. Now only remains the task of entering into the adventure fully prepared. Preparation in this case means being ready physically, emotionally and spiritually.

It doesn't take much to get physically prepared for a Day of Reflection. Mainly, it's a matter of wearing comfortable clothes, and if any part of your day will be spent outside, you will need to take weather conditions into consideration in your choice of clothes and outerwear. It is also important to give some thought to your food and beverage needs. Even if your Day of Reflection will take place at home, it is good to have decided what you will eat and drink and to have these commodities either prepared beforehand or able to be easily prepared when you are ready to consume them. Because of the nature of a Day of Reflection, food and drink considerations should actually be of relative unimportance. It is quite common, in fact, to fast during or in preparation for this time.

Emotionally, it is good to recognize the importance of the time you are dedicating to a Day of Reflection and to anticipate its special nature. In a way, every day is a new adventure; as a friend of mine says, "Each day has its own personality." Therefore, make your Day of Reflection special by dedicating it solely to you and God. Do this by not planning or scheduling anything of any importance for the day. Thus, intend that your Day of Reflection be a true "sabbath." (The word "sabbath" means "stop work," and our concept of sabbatical comes from this root. Additional reference to stopping work and the Sabbath can be found under *Resting* on page 34.)

The best spiritual preparation you can engage in for a Day of Reflection is prayer. Pray to God that you will indeed be able to put aside the distracting thoughts and mundane concerns of your life for a while. Pray for the ability to be open to hearing and understanding God's communication. Pray that you will be open to receiving and acting upon the wisdom of God's Holy Spirit. Finally, pray a prayer of thanks simply for being able to spend the upcoming time in God's presence.

Chapter Two
Experiencing a Day of Reflection

*A*ctually *experiencing a Day of Reflection is something so personal and varied that it is impossible to speak about it in general terms.*

A recent visitor to Shalom House came for two nights and found simply that resting, time away from the demands of three children and a husband, as well as an opportunity to write Christmas cards, provided a wonderful recharging of her spiritual life.

The following is one person's account of how she plans and carries out a Day of Reflection:

Beth often decides to engage in a Day of Reflection

when there is something on her mind and she needs the space and time to think. She blocks off an entire day (9 to 5). Sometimes she looks for a little class to take, like yoga; other times she starts off by simply sitting in a nearby church for a while. She likes to spend part of her day at a nature area, but if there are too many people there, she'll just go off and sit by a river or stream.

Beth enjoys going someplace and seeing what happens. She says that a big part of the day is just being spontaneous. She believes it is important to be flexible, to let your feelings come up. For her, a Day of Reflection is like "being with your soul, which is always so hidden and buried." She strongly believes that if you give yourself time, you will get answers.

Later, on Beth's Days of Reflection, she ends up exploring neighborhoods, museums, bookstores or music stores. She says the days provide her with self-esteem; through them she learns to have fun by herself. According to Beth, "If everyone did this, our world would be transformed."

Here is how Beth characterizes her special days:

Days of Reflection
To notice the little things
To walk a little slower
To hear the dogs bark, the birds chirp

To treasure the sunshine
To look into the sky
To introduce yourself to yourself
To listen
To play
To accept unpredictable invitations
To stretch and relax in the calm of your soul and your God
Before returning to the structure and time of everyday.
—Beth Ebner

I've often thought that, for a Day of Reflection, I'd sometime like to take time to do nothing but follow one of my cats around. Cats seem to know exactly how to live in the present moment, and they certainly know a lot about the value of rest!

This section includes a range of things to do (and sometimes to refrain from doing) on your own Day of Reflection. While consideration of which activities you want to include in your Day of Reflection is a part of the planning process for the day, I decided to include the activities here as a section about the day itself. Thus, as you enter into what you have planned, you will know that you are free, either to do things differently from what you had originally designed, or perhaps to spend more time on something that you find particularly helpful as you experience the day. Be mindful, however, that your main task is to *listen* to God, and that all the activities of your Day of Reflection should be designed in order to bring this about.

Keeping Silent

> Silence is deep as Eternity.
>
> —Thomas Carlyle

What better way to listen than to be silent? Maintaining silence is, in fact, a traditional retreat practice. Of course, if you are alone at home on your Day of Reflection, this is fairly easy to do. If, however, you decide to spend your day at a retreat house and there are other retreatants present, more effort will be required on your part to keep silent. No one, most of all the retreat house director, will find your silence odd, and, of course, we are not talking about going to extremes. For example, questions as to the location of rooms or outside sites need to be asked, and pleasant, brief greetings to others are certainly appropriate.

There are sound reasons why maintaining silence is of assistance on a Day of Reflection. First, since the whole idea is to get away from the usual occurrences of everyday life, not having to hear chitchat is a real luxury. We are social creatures by nature, and much of our conversing is ultimately unimportant. Its purpose is to keep us in communion, in relation to others in our lives. Therefore, in the morning it is only natural to inquire of family members, "Did you sleep well?" or to relate a funny dream one had. Similarly, we go to work on Monday and invariably someone asks, "What did you do this weekend?" Not to engage in this social chatter would be quite abnormal. On a Day of Reflection, though, there is simply no reason for this unimportant talk.

A second reason for silence is that it allows communications from God to enter our soul. Sometimes people—consciously or unconsciously—surround themselves with people and activities all their waking hours so as not to confront their God in the stillness of their souls. In staying engaged with others or simply remaining busy all the time, they trick themselves into thinking that they are most perfectly carrying out God's will through their acts of service to family and neighbors. While, indeed, God's Spirit frequently speaks to us through others in our lives, it is very important that we listen for and hear clear messages sent directly to our minds, hearts and souls by God.

A third reason for maintaining silence, particularly if your day or a part of it is spent outside, is that in turning our attention away from thoughts and their utterance, we are so much more open to the true experience of God's universe—its many and diverse sights, sounds, smells and physical feelings. We become less the cerebral, thinking creatures that we tend to be most of the time, and more experiential, childlike, sensual beings, rooted to the earth and an actual part of God's creation.

Fasting

> When the stomach is full, it is easy to talk of fasting.
>
> —St. Jerome

The discipline of fasting was alluded to earlier in planning for a day of reflection. Fasting, like maintaining silence, is another traditional spiritual practice; probably its most well-known example is Jesus' fasting for forty days in the desert. Fasting is not a popular experience in our Western world of instant physical gratification: prepared food is in abundance, and grocery stores stay open all night to meet our consumer demand for bodily satisfaction. Even the Catholic Church, which once required a degree of fasting by its members during the holy season of Lent, now only requires adults to fast (i.e., a limit of one substantial meal, two smaller ones and no other food) on Ash Wednesday and Good Friday. (The Church still continues, however, to encourage fasting between meals as a Lenten sacrificial observance.)

Nonetheless, fasting as a spiritual discipline in both Eastern and Western traditions is pursued as a form of purification of the physical body. In briefly giving up the natural pleasures associated with eating, those who fast are, in a sense, "training" themselves for the spiritual journey similar to the way athletes exercise and avoid certain foods in training for special athletic events. When we train our bodies to refrain from physical pleasure, we are simply more able to concentrate on matters of the spirit and more able to listen to God's word to us.

It is a good idea to try out the practice of fasting on your Day of Reflection, either by taking only fluids as bodily nourishment or by eating more lightly than usual. If you find that it does indeed make your Day of Reflection more of a spiritual exercise, continue to incorporate the practice into future Days of Reflection. If you do not feel a positive effect from fasting and instead are distracted by your hunger, there is no sense in continuing to fast.

Praying

> Pray without ceasing.
>
> —Colossians 5:17

Books and books have been written on the spiritual exercise of prayer. Put simply, however, the definition of prayer is the lifting of one's heart and mind to God in order to be in relationship with God.

Prayer puts us in touch with the Almighty, Universal Goodness. Praying is an excellent way for us to step out of our narrow, bounded human nature and to experience profoundly that spark of God's divinity resident within our immortal souls.

To pray is to both talk and listen—true communication. So, after you've gone through all you've planned to say to God (praise, thanks, petitions for oneself and others, requests for divine guidance and the will to carry it out), then *listen!*

There is a story about a man who went to visit his minister and, upon being met at the door by the minister's wife, was told, "He is busy; he is praying." The man could quite distinctly hear the minister's words of praise and petition, so he said he'd return the next day. The following day, the man came by and once again was told the minister was busy praying. The minister's pleas and words of adoration were again very audible, so once more the man told the minister's wife he'd return the next day. On the third day, the man asked to see the minister and was told again that the minister was busy praying. Hearing once more words of prayer and supplication, the man said he'd return yet again the next day. This time, though, he also said to the minister's wife, "Please remind your husband, 'God is a gentleman: He doesn't interrupt.'"

In your own prayer time, therefore, *spend at least as much time listening as you have speaking.* Listening in the context of prayer is an active listening, a sort of waiting on the Lord, particularly when you are seeking something specific, for example, guidance or direction. Be ready and open, though, to hear what you're not expecting or, for that matter, to hear nothing at all! God's goodness is so profound and timeless that we can never know its fullness nor when it will be revealed to us.

Some may find it difficult to design their own prayers to God. If the pressure or inconvenience of self-initiated prayers becomes so cumbersome that it keeps you away from prayer, feel free to use standard prayers that you know or consult any of the vast number of prayer books available to spiritual seekers. Another aid to prayer is a rosary or other types of prayer beads.

The best place in which to engage in prayer is a quiet place that is free of distraction. You will be led to where the best place is for you.

Meditating

> Let the words of my mouth and the meditation of my heart be acceptable in thy sight, O Lord, my strength and my redeemer.
>
> —Psalms 19:14

Where there is peace and meditation, there is neither anxiety nor doubt.

—St. Francis of Assisi

There are probably as many definitions of meditation as there are of prayer. Essentially, meditation is removing conscious thought from your mind as a way of experiencing God's presence or of opening yourself to the inspiration of God's Spirit. In short, *meditating allows us to listen.*

We are not used to having our minds devoid of thought. Many of us are so disciplined that we don't even allow ourselves the pleasure of daydreaming. To engage in meditation, one generally repeats to oneself a mantra, a word or sound of no particular meaning, which helps remove oneself from the thinking process. It is well to remember, though, that thoughts inherently occur, and in meditation we don't fight their natural intrusion; we simply pay thoughts no heed—by not dwelling on them.

Those who meditate often pay attention to the regular inhalation and exhalation of their breath. Some people, in fact, combine attention to their breath with the recitation of a brief prayer or invocation such as, "Come, Creator Spirit." Other ways of entering into a state of meditation include contemplating something, for example, an object of nature either in the wild or brought in from outside, or concentrating on the flame of a candle.

The practice of meditation helps us to center ourselves, to come to a place of peace and refreshment away from the concerns that constantly preoccupy our minds.

Although preferred by many, meditation in a prayer room or chapel is not the only way to engage in this practice. Many retreatants have told me that they do their best meditating in a boat on the pond with a fishing pole in hand!

Listening to tapes (or CDs)

> You do not need to leave your room. Remain sitting at your table and listen. Do not even listen, simply wait. Do not even wait, be still and solitary.
> —Franz Kafka

Some people pray or meditate more easily with background music. Certainly music is an integral part of the liturgical celebrations of many religions. Music for a Day of Reflection may take many forms: classical music in general; organ music; more religious music, such as Gregorian chant, Taizé, the music of Hildegarde of Bingen; or even the currently popular combination of classical music and jazz.

While not exactly considered "music," there are several kinds of tapes that include nature sounds, such as pounding ocean, soft rain, nighttime pond frogs, and so on. These sounds are very relaxing and would be especially appreciated if your entire Day of Reflection is spent indoors.

Other kinds of tapes that may be enjoyed on a Day of Reflection are those of the spoken word. There are tapes available as an aid to meditation or relaxation. In addition, books-on-tape are becoming increasingly popular, as are the taped proceedings of spiritual conferences or retreats.

Reading

> Reading is to the mind what exercise is to the body.
>
> —Sir Richard Steele

> Live always in the best company when you read.
>
> —Sydney Smith

A Day of Reflection is an excellent opportunity for reading. Reading material may be as diverse as the Bible or the latest self-help book. Any material that is inspirational to your heart and soul is good to spend time with on a Day of Reflection. As examples, I have included a list of titles that I would recommend for reading on a Day of Reflection at the end of this book (Appendix B).

Resting

> Come unto me, all ye that labor and are heavy laden, and I will give you rest.
>
> —Matthew 11:28

When was the last time you took a midday nap? While this may not seem like an appropriate activity for a Day of Reflection, what better way for us to shift gears and make a smooth transition to a period of time with no deadlines or demands? The very act of engaging in something so outside our daily experience as resting facilitates our movement to deeper realms of ourselves.

Resting does not necessarily even mean sleeping. It can be nothing more than sitting and daydreaming in a comfortable chair or in the middle of a flowering meadow.

The idea of resting is so sacred that the Book of Genesis tells us that our God even rested from the labors of creation. What a wonderful model for our weary selves! Not only is the idea of resting presented to us as an excellent example to follow, but also as we read later in the Hebrew scriptures, God goes a step further with the concept of rest by including it among one of the Ten Commandments!

> Remember the sabbath day and keep it holy. For six days you shall labor and do all your work but the seventh day is a sabbath for Yahweh your God. You shall do no work that day, neither you nor your son nor your daughter, not your servants, men or women, nor your animals nor the stranger who lives with you. For in six days Yahweh made the heavens and the earth and the sea and all that these hold, but on the seventh day he rested; that is why Yahweh has blessed the sabbath day and made it sacred.
>
> —Exodus 20: 8–11

(It occurred to me as I wrote this section that if we all took the Third Commandment a little more seriously, there would probably not be such a need for Days of Reflection—or for that matter, for any kind of spiritual retreats!)

What it comes down to is that doing nothing is a wonderful luxury, and when doing nothing, you're giving

God the perfect opportunity to speak to you. On a Day of Reflection it's quite all right to do nothing; for example, it's okay to take a boat out into the middle of a pond and not even fish!

Listening for God's wisdom in the context of rest and relaxation is more passive but no less significant than the listening that you engage in within the context of prayer. Listening while doing nothing is a matter of simply being open to God, to God's word and to God's will.

Writing

> I know what I know and I write it.
>
> —Octavio Paz

Writing is an excellent activity for a Day of Reflection, perhaps because it is something we engage in so rarely in our everyday lives. A cloth-covered, blank book is a wonderful accompaniment to a Day of Reflection, or, for that matter, any sort of notebook would serve the purpose.

What to write? A Day of Reflection seems to be a good time to do just that—reflect on what you hear God saying to you in the stillness of your soul, or perhaps reflect on what you are reading this day.

You may find it easier praying to God by writing down your thoughts. An advantage to this form of prayer is that you can go back and use the prayers over and over, creating in time your own unique prayer book.

A Day of Reflection is a good opportunity to try one's hand at poetry. A simple form of poetry and one that I encourage retreatants to engage in during seasonal

Days of Reflection is haiku. Haiku uses the medium of ordinary language, and its subject matter concerns the contemplation of natural objects in the present moment. Often there are allusions to the season, location or time of day. Writers are encouraged to write poems of three lines, with a total of approximately seventeen syllables, and rhyming is, in fact, discouraged! Here is a haiku poem written by one of the participants at a spring Day of Reflection:

> Rain dapples the pond
> As new Spring growth emerges.
> We walk together.
> —Rita McGovern

If you have never begun a journal or are not journaling at present, a Day of Reflection is an appropriate occasion to begin or return to this time-honored practice. To go back after a period of time and review our journal entries is a way to measure and chart progress on our spiritual pilgrimage. Don't let the imagined burden of daily entries be an obstacle to starting a journal: some days there just won't be either time to make an entry or anything of value to say. No problem. Just as often there will be so much to reflect on that it will be impossible to record it all!

Finally, writing might also take the form of letters to friends and relatives. Can one possibly overstate the joy felt from receiving a handwritten letter? Perhaps it is time to return the favor or simply to surprise a loved one with a note or letter. You might even think of brief notes to friends and relatives as "postcards" from your minivacation of a Day of Reflection. Maybe in the process, you will inspire the recipients of your communications to take such a day for themselves....

Walking

> Happily may I walk.
> May it be beautiful before me.
> May it be beautiful behind me.
> May it be beautiful below me.
> May it be beautiful above me.
> May it be beautiful all around me.
> —Navaho Night Chant

It is hard to overstate the worth of walking on a Day of Reflection as an aid to one's prayer or meditation. The utter simplicity of putting one foot in front of the other with no particular destination or time schedule is a most restful background into which one can invite God's Spirit. Since walking involves no particular skill or heavy exertion, we are free to give ourselves over to listening to God's inspiration.

Aside from being healthy exercise, walking puts us in touch with and thus makes us immediately aware and appreciative of the magnificence of God's creation. The nice thing about walking is that it can be done in whatever setting you have chosen for your Day of Reflection. Even if your walking is not along a country meadow or a shady path in the woods, it is still likely there will be a range of flora and fauna along the way that you have never seen before or bird songs and insect noises you have never heard. One's neighborhood can reveal all sorts of wonders if one is open to their appreciation!

Another nice thing about walking is that, provided you have sufficient outer gear, the weather does not have to be an obstacle to enjoying the outside. God's presence in the world is perceived just as clearly on a snowy evening or a rainy afternoon.

As I was finishing this book while on a Christmas retreat at Transfiguration Monastery in southern New York State, I experienced the most wonderful peace and tranquility while hiking the mountain against which the monastery is situated. The temperature was mild for the time of year and location, and it had been gently but steadily raining (no surprise here, I daresay!) all morning. I set out for my third day's hike along the monastery's very well-marked and well-tended trails. I was warmly dressed, wearing hiking boots, a hooded down-filled coat and accompanied by a steady walking stick.

Toward the summit of the mountain, beneath tall pines swaying and singing in the light rain, I felt such an immense closeness with God, a feeling close to what I have heard others describe as their feeling of intimacy with Christ in the eucharist. A little later, across my path in the distance ran five or six white-tailed deer. At such times (and we can never engineer them—only be open to their experience), God is surely speaking of the wonders of creation and is giving just a taste of the afterlife prepared for those who earnestly try to seek God's will for their lives. *Deo gracias.*

> For Satan finds some mischief still
> For idle hands to do.
> > —Isaac Watts
> > "Against Idleness and Mischief,"
> > from *Divine Songs*

> Work is love made visible.
> > —Kahlil Gibran
> > "On Work,"
> > from *The Prophet*

Engaging in crafts or handiwork on a Day of Reflection can include a broad range of activities. On seasonal Days of Reflection I have encouraged participants to work in the media of clay or watercolor as avenues of self-expression. A Day of Reflection is a perfect opportunity to devote to handiwork projects for which there is rarely enough time in the course of everyday life. Also, like walking, engaging in projects like knitting, needlework or carving serves as a restful background during periods of prayer or meditation. It is an excellent time to listen for and to the promptings of God's Spirit.

Chapter Three

Remembering Your Day of Reflection

All too quickly, your Day of Reflection will come to an end. Before you jump back into all of your regular activities, it might be a good idea to plan your next spiritual getaway. It seems important to most people to have something to look forward to beyond the joys and cares of everyday life. Having now experienced a Day of Reflection, you have some ideas as to how you might want to improve a future one: experiencing it in a different location, doing more, or less, of various activities, and so on.

If your day even partially met your expectations, it is probable that you'd like to retain a sense of the peace

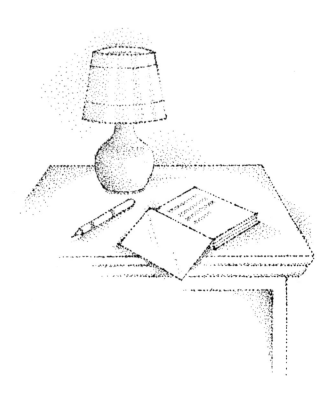

and calmness you've experienced. To do this and as a way of keeping yourself nurtured till the next time, consider incorporating a piece of two of the day's activities into your day-to-day life.

This may be done as easily as committing to a regular period of journaling every day or an evening walk around the neighborhood. Setting aside a particular amount of time each day for prayer or meditation, reading or letter writing is a nice enhancement to ordinary routine.

Finally, if your life seems just too chaotic or chockfull of responsibilities to spouse, children, elderly parents, employer, pets or home maintenance to incorporate even one more activity, do try just one simple carry-over from your Day of Reflection. Have a little notepad and pen by your bed, and every night before turning out the light, record the day's date and note one thing (or more if they come easily to mind) from the day for which you're thankful to God. (A small calendar with a space for every day would work fine, too.) In time, you will have your own "thanksgiving litany" and, above all, a reminder that even when our lives are so fast-paced that we hardly feel we have time for God, we will see at a glance how good and gracious God is to us every one of our days upon this earth.

Appendix A
Sample Schedules for a Day of Reflection

My first "draft" of this section included just the first sample schedule. Feedback from many friends and colleagues, however, demonstrated that people have varying degrees of need for structure, so I have included as samples both a highly and a loosely structured Day of Reflection.

Day of Reflection: Sample schedule I

This is a *sample* for those who appreciate a more structured approach to the day. It includes a little of most of the activities described in chapter 2. If it is your first time planning and carrying out a Day of Reflection, you will probably find this sample helpful.

9:00   Begin your day in quiet prayer, asking God to send the Spirit to your heart, mind and soul, that you may be renewed spiritually and emotionally. Consider, too, being specific about things you want or need out of this day.

9:10   Having prayed, take several deep breaths and enter into a period of deep meditation. Use a favorite mantra or invocation, pay attention to breathing or place concentration on a candle's flame.

9:40   Take a long walk, exploring the outdoor environment. Even in a city, as you walk *be aware* and listen for sounds you've never heard; look at things to which you've never paid any attention; touch things you've never felt; smell scents you've never smelled before.

10:30   Take a tea or juice break.

10:45   Read.

11:30   Write a few letters, answering some you've let "sit" for a while as well as surprising a friend or two with a note from you that they hadn't expected.

Afternoon

12:30   Pray, first thanking God for all you've been given, then asking God to answer your own and others' intentions; finally, listen in the depths of your soul for messages or directions God may be telling you.

1:15   Have a light lunch of cheese, crackers and yogurt or soup and bread.

1:30   Start or continue a journal about your experiences today, including how you planned this special day (i.e., what made you choose the date, the location, what you're reading, who you're writing to and so on).

2:15   Another walk, perhaps retracing your first walk, but from the other direction, allowing yourself to experience something of the familiar, but from a new perspective.

3:15   Afternoon tea or juice break.

3:30   Work on a needlework, knitting or carving project, or on your own favorite handwork.

5:00   Prepare to depart: gather books, writing materials, crafts; decide when your next Day of Reflection will occur (even if it's this same date next year).

5:15   Spend your final portion of time with God in thanksgiving for the precious time you enjoyed today; once again, listen deeply for God's word; record in your journal the thoughts and intuitions you've received now and throughout the day.

Day of Reflection: Sample schedule II

There is much merit to the idea that the less you do on a Day of Reflection, the more likely you are to hear God. Sometimes schedules can get in the way!

Initial activities	Spend time in quiet meditation, listening carefully to your soul for the formation of questions for which you will seek answers today.
	Read or pray.
Midmorning	Take a tea or juice break.
Late morning	Listen to music.
	Spend more time in quiet meditation, listening to your soul for guidance, or maybe more questions.
Early afternoon	Eat a light lunch.
	Take a walk, allowing God's Spirit to lead you.
Midafternoon	Take a nap.
Late afternoon	Write a letter to God.

Appendix B
Suggested Reading for a Day of Reflection

Craven, Margaret. *I Heard the Owl Call My Name*. Garden City, NY: Doubleday, 1973.

Green, Thomas H. *Opening to God: A Guide to Prayer*. Notre Dame, IN: Ave Maria Press, 1977.

Hays, Edward M. *St. George and the Dragon and the Quest for the Holy Grail*. Easton, KS: Forest of Peace Books, 1986.

Moore, Thomas. *Care of the Soul: A Guide for Cultivating Depth and Sacredness in Everyday Life*. New York: HarperCollins, 1992.

Nouwen, Henri J. M. *In Memoriam*. Notre Dame, IN: Ave Maria Press, 1980.

Peck, M. Scott. *The Road Less Traveled: A New Psychology of*

Love, Traditional Values and Spiritual Growth. New York: Simon & Schuster, 1978.

Shannon, William Henry. *Silence on Fire: The Prayer of Awareness.* New York: Crossroad, 1991.

St. Thérèse of Lisieux. *Story of a Soul: The Autobiography of St. Thérèse of Lisieux.* Washington: ICS Publications, 1976.

ILLUMINATIONBOOKS

Other Books in the Series

Little Pieces of Light...Darkness and Personal Growth
by Joyce Rupp

Lessons from the Monastery That Touch Your Life
by M. Basil Pennington, O.C.S.O.

As You and the Abused Person Journey Together
by Sharon E. Cheston

Spirituality, Stress & You
by Thomas E. Rodgerson

Joy, The Dancing Spirit of Love Surrounding You
by Beverly Elaine Eanes

Every Decision You Make Is a Spiritual One
by Anthony J. De Conciliis with John F. Kinsella

Celebrating the Woman You Are
by S. Suzanne Mayer, I.H.M.

Why Are You Worrying?
by Joseph W. Ciarrocchi

Partners in the Divine Dance of Our Three Person'd God
by Shaun McCarty, S.T.

Love God...Clean House...Help Others
by Duane F. Reinert, O.F.M. Cap.

Along Your Desert Journey
by Robert M. Hamma

Appreciating God's Creation Through Scripture
by Alice L. Laffey

Let Yourself Be Loved
by Phillip Bennett

Facing Discouragement
by Kathleen Fischer and Thomas Hart

Living Simply in an Anxious World
by Robert J. Wicks